1

Moses Marketing

(Learning to market yourself from someone who thought he was inadequate)

Drew Wohlford

Introduction

Moses thought he was under qualified to lead God showed him differently He survived one of the great child massacres in the Bible He was a potential candidate to succeed Pharaoh He had a stuttering problem He had to relearn things in the wilderness for forty years

Moses Marketing is a name that has been given to this project because of certain characteristics

Moses had. Moses thought he was under qualified but God showed him differently. He survived one of the great child massacres in the Bible, He was a potential candidate to succeed Pharaoh, and had a stuttering problem going to show you how to use Moses' life to market yourself.

Moses was a normal Israelite boy who struggled with speech, but God used his life to appeal to people. If you always know what's going on in the world and make sure your friends do too, be like Moses.

Moses Marketing is a way of using the life of Moses to market yourself. Moses was in many ways the ultimate underdog, who had to beat all odds and prove himself worthy and capable of doing the job at hand.

Moses was born in slavery and at age 40 he killed a slave master for beating a Hebrew in front of him. Moses then fled to Midian, where he met his wife

Zipporah. Moses returned to Egypt 40 years later, as God ordered him to do so, and was given leprosy after killing an Egyptian for beating a Hebrew slave. After being cured by God, Moses returned to lead the Israelites across the Red Sea on dry land and into Sinai where God gave them the Ten Commandments on Mt. Sinai. Moses died at age 120, full of days but healthy until his last moment on this earth.

Moses was an unlikely hero.For 40 years he begged God to allow him to lead the Israelites out of Egypt and into their new homeland. People didn't listen to Moses because they found him to be stiff-necked and hard to work with. But God picked this unlikely man—a murderer who didn't know right from wrong—to lead His chosen people out of bondage and into freedom."

Moses was a leader in an era when leading people was not easy. Despite his disabilities, he still managed to become one of the great leaders of the Bible. You too have the opportunity to learn from Moses' life. Learn his faults and weaknesses, but also learn how he overcame them for God's purpose.

Never let your weaknesses cause you to stop dreaming. Moses was a powerful leader, yet he stuttered. He thought he was not good enough to lead the Israelites out of Egypt, but God told him otherwise by giving him the 10 commandments on Mount Sinai.

When God first calls Moses out of obscurity, he believes he is unqualified to do the job. But God shows him otherwise and—after miraculously escaping death at the hands of Pharaoh's men—Moses becomes the man tasked with leading a million people out of slavery and up Mount Sinai for 40 years' worth of lessons from God on the tablets. He eventually marries into royalty, has a speech problem that he overcomes, leads Israel toward their new homeland despite constant opposition, fights in war after war against his people's enemies and goes on to die at age 120—a ripe old age for those days. Here are seven things you didn't know about this fantastic man of God.

Moses was born into slavery, but God would not let him remain in it. At a young age, Moses killed an Egyptian who had beaten an Israelite slave. For this crime he was exiled for life to Midian as punishment. There, one day while shepherding his father-in-law's flocks of sheep, a divine messenger appeared to him in a burning bush and called upon him to go back to Egypt and lead the Israelites out of their long bondage under Pharaoh

In Exodus, we see God at work through Moses. The story is filled with twists and turns, characters who fail and rise again, impossibilities overcome, miracles performed—and a sense that God has been preparing this extraordinary moment for thousands of years. Not only does God use Moses to lead the Israelites out of slavery, he also guides him through forty years in the wilderness to prepare for his ministry as a prophet.

Moses was a man who had a speech defect going to show you how to use moses life to market yourself he came from the priestly tribe and was not perfect he died at a good old age (120) but he was totally healthy

From a young boy called out of nowhere to lead his people out of slavery to an old man crossing the Red Sea after 40 years, Moses was the central figure in Israel's history. Yet despite this fame and notoriety, Moses was a private person who (apart from some petty spying expeditions) only appeared on stage when needed. He was no angel; he had a speech problem, needed lessons in leadership and endured many failures leading up to his great success. So how did he make it through? Like all of us who suffer from low self-esteem, I was told early in life that I wasn't qualified for the position I've been assigned in God's Kingdom. My story is similar to Moses' in this regard as well. But like Moses, after my fatherhood training skills proved inadequate (as seen with Aaron's sons), I asked God for help. And none came initially because I didn't feel worthy enough! Instead of hiding behind my problems, though, I overcame them both by possessing faith in God's promises and speaking boldly those promises out loud —

just like Moses did. Today there is finally hope for others who feel they are not good enough or don't have what it takes because our Father has already revealed Himself to each

Moses was a meek man, but he was persistent. When God calls you to do something—even if it doesn't make sense or seems impossible—He will equip you with just the right skills and talents!

As a Brand and Marketing professional, one of the greatest gifts that I have received has always been the ability to see things in a new way. After all, following the masses while engaging in groupthink is not beneficial when it comes to creating brands & marketing strategies that stand out above the rest.

What Is Job Searching

Moses was a man of faith who had been called to lead the Israelites out of bondage in Egypt. He had been chosen by God to be the leader of the Israelites out of Egypt and into the promised land. As such, Moses had to be a leader of men and had to find the right people to help him in his mission.

In the same way, when you are looking for a job, you must be a leader of yourself and of the process. You must search out the right job for you and take the necessary steps to land the job. Moses had to search for the right people to follow him and help him on his mission. He had to be diligent in his search and make sure that he was bringing the right people along with him.

The same is true when you are job searching. You must be thorough in your search. You must look for the right job fit for you and take the necessary steps to land the job. You must make sure that you are sending your resume to the right companies and the right people. You must also prepare for the interviews and be sure to present yourself in the best light.

Moses had to be patient and persistent in his search for the right people to follow him. He had to be patient with the process and keep looking until he found the right people. The same is true when job searching. You must be patient and persistent in your search. You must look for the right job fit for you and take the necessary steps to land the job.

Moses was a leader of men and was able to find the right people to follow him and help him in his mission. In the same way, when you are job searching, you must be a leader of yourself and of the process. You must search out the right job fit for you and take the necessary steps to land the job. You must be patient and persistent and make sure that you are bringing the right people along with you.

Be sure to network with the right contacts and use the right resources. Leverage the skills and knowledge you have and identify the skills gap that you need to fill to ensure that you're prepared for the job you're looking for.

Research the company and the position, and make sure you're ready to go in for the interview. Make sure you have a plan and a strategy for the job search process and don't give up until you've landed the job.

As you embark on your job search journey, don't forget to take care of yourself. Make sure you're eating right, sleeping enough, exercising, and taking time to relax. This will help you stay focused and energized, so you can stay on track in your job search. Additionally, remember that job searching can be a long process. There will be times when you feel discouraged or overwhelmed, but don't forget to stay positive and keep your eye on the prize.

Take the time to celebrate the small successes along the way, like when you land an interview or when you get a job offer. These successes will motivate you and help you stay focused on your long-term goals.

Overview Of The Process

Moses was a great leader, but he was also a man of the people. He knew the importance of finding a job and providing for his family. In this chapter, Moses will be our guide as we explore the job searching process.

The first step in the job searching process is to create a resume. A resume is a document that outlines your experience, skills, and education. Moses was a skilled orator and leader, so he would have been sure to highlight his skills in this area. He also likely would have included a list of his accomplishments, such as leading the Israelites out of Egypt.

The next step is to start searching for job openings. Moses would have done this by looking in the local markets and talking to other people in the community. He would have looked for positions that matched his skills and experience.

Once you have found potential job openings, it's time to apply. Moses would have made sure to follow any instructions that were provided. This could include writing a cover letter, submitting a job application, or providing references.

Once you have applied, it's time to wait for a response. Moses would have been patient and waited to hear back from potential employers. He would have followed up if he had not heard back after a certain amount of time.

If you are selected for an interview, it's time to prepare. Moses would have taken the time to really think about the questions he was likely to be asked. He would have also taken the time to practice his answers and to dress appropriately for the interview.

Finally, it's time to negotiate a salary. Moses would have taken the time to research the average salary for the position and would have been sure to advocate for himself. He would have also been sure to negotiate for any benefits that he felt were important.

No matter where you are in the job searching process, Moses would have reminded you to stay patient and positive. He knew that finding a job was not easy, but with hard work and dedication, it could be done.

Moses would have also reminded you to stay organized. He would have recommended that you keep a list of the jobs you applied for, the date you applied, and any follow-up activities. He would also encourage you to keep track of your contacts and the conversations you had with them. In addition, he would have suggested that you take time to practice interviewing skills and make sure that you have a good understanding of the company and the position for which you are applying.

Finally, Moses would have encouraged you to stay motivated throughout the process. He would have reminded you that you have something valuable to offer, and to believe in yourself and your abilities. He would have encouraged you to take time to celebrate any successes, no matter how small, and to hang on to hope in the face of challenges.

Moses was a great believer in the power of preparation. He would have encouraged you to create a system for yourself that would help you to stay organized throughout the job search process. He would have suggested that you set aside time each day to devote to searching for jobs, researching companies, and networking. He would have also advised you to make sure you had an updated resume and cover letter ready to go.

Perfect Resume

Moses was a leader and a man of great faith. His life story is filled with examples of how he used his skill and determination to achieve his goals. This makes him an excellent example of how to create the perfect resume. The following elements should be included in a resume to emulate Moses' success:

1. Education: Moses was a gifted leader and scholar. As such, it is important to include a detailed list of all educational qualifications. Include any degrees or certifications, as well as any special awards or honors.

2. Skills and Abilities: Moses was a masterful leader and negotiator. To emulate this, list any relevant skills and abilities on the resume. This could include public speaking, problem solving, or negotiation abilities.

3. Work Experience: Moses had a long and varied history of leading and managing people. This should be reflected on the resume, including a list of any positions held and any accomplishments achieved in those roles.

4. Community Involvement: Moses was a leader in the community. List any volunteer work or involvement in any local groups or organizations.

5. Leadership: Moses was a natural leader. Include any examples of how you have exhibited leadership in your

career, such as leading a project or managing a team.

By including these elements in a resume, a job seeker can emulate the success of Moses and position themselves for success.

Moses demonstrated his leadership skills through his involvement in various organizations. He was a founding member of the local church, and was instrumental in organizing community events and fundraisers. He also served as a board member for a local non-profit organization, and was responsible for helping to create structure and guidelines for the organization. In addition, he served as a mentor to numerous young people in the community, providing guidance and leadership through difficult times.

Dress For Success

The biblical character of Moses is perhaps best known for leading the Israelites out of Egypt and into the Promised Land. However, his wisdom extends beyond the realm of religion and into the world of professional success. In this chapter, we will explore how Moses's advice on dressing for a job interview can help you make a great first impression and secure the job of your dreams.

When preparing for a job interview, it is important to dress appropriately. While there is no single "right" way to dress, Moses cautions us to err on the side of caution. In Exodus 28:42, he writes: "And you shall make for them linen breeches to cover their nakedness; they shall reach from the waist to the thighs." This passage reminds us that it is important to dress modestly, and to avoid clothing that is too revealing or inappropriate for the workplace.

Moses also emphasizes the importance of neatness and grooming. In Leviticus 19:19, he writes: "You shall keep my statutes. You shall not let your livestock breed with a different kind. You shall not sow your field with two kinds of seed, nor shall you wear a garment of cloth made of two kinds of material." This passage teaches us that it is important to take care in our appearance and to make sure that our clothing is neat and well-fitted. It also reminds us to be mindful of the colors and fabrics we choose, and to avoid clothing that is too loud or bright.

Finally, Moses advises us to be mindful of the message that our clothing sends. In

Deuteronomy 22:5, he writes: "A woman shall not wear a man's garment, nor shall a man put on a woman's cloak, for whoever does these things is an abomination to the Lord your God." This passage encourages us to dress in a manner that is appropriate for the job we are interviewing for, and to avoid clothing that sends inappropriate messages or is overly suggestive.

It is also important to remember that clothing is more than just a way to express ourselves. It can also be used as a tool to show respect for others and to honor God. We should take care to choose clothing that is modest and appropriate for the occasion, and to avoid anything that could be interpreted as disrespectful or dishonoring. By taking the time to be mindful of our wardrobe choices, we can honor God and show respect to those around us.

Additionally, clothing can be used to send a message of acceptance and inclusion. By wearing clothing that is representative of different cultures and backgrounds, we can show respect to those with different backgrounds or experiences. This kind of clothing can also be used to show solidarity with a particular community or to raise awareness about important issues. By taking the time to consider our clothing choices, we can show our support for those in need and demonstrate our commitment to justice.

Furthermore, clothing can be used to express our individuality and creativity. By choosing clothes that express our unique personality, we can show the world who we are and what we stand for. This kind of clothing can be a powerful tool to express our values and beliefs, and can also be used to make a statement about the kind of world we want to live in. By expressing ourselves through clothing, we can create a more positive and inclusive environment.

By following the advice of Moses, you can make sure that you are well-dressed and prepared for any job interview. Remember to dress modestly, to take care in your grooming, and to choose clothing that is appropriate for the job. With the wisdom of Moses in mind, you will be sure to make a great first impression and secure the job of your dreams.

Pick The Right Outfit

The bible tells us that Moses was a great leader who commanded the Israelites from the bondage of slavery in Egypt to the promised land. However, Moses was not only a great leader, he was also a great fashionista. He knew how to pick out the perfect outfit for any occasion.

Moses understood that when it comes to picking out the right outfit, the most important thing is to be comfortable in what you wear. He believed that when you feel comfortable in your clothing, it can help to boost your confidence and make you stand out from the crowd.

When it comes to finding the right outfit, Moses suggests starting with the basics. He recommends investing in a few key pieces that can be easily mixed and matched to create a variety of looks. A good pair of jeans, a classic white shirt, and a well-made blazer are some of his favorite items to have in his wardrobe.

Moses also advises that when it comes to accessorizing, less is more. He believes that a few statement pieces can make all the difference in an outfit. A pair of striking earrings or a bold necklace can really elevate a look and make it look more sophisticated.

Moses was also a fan of color. He often chose to wear bright colors to show off his personality and stand out from the crowd. He often advised his followers to choose bright colors to show off their individual style.

Moses was also a big believer in mixing and matching different colors and patterns to create a unique look. He encouraged his followers to experiment and be creative to find the perfect combination of colors and patterns that suited their individual style. He believed that being daring and daring to be different was the key to creating a look that was truly one-of-a-kind.

Finally, Moses believed that the most important thing when getting dressed was to have fun. He encouraged his followers to experiment with different styles and colors and to not be afraid to express themselves through their clothing.

Moses was a great leader and a great fashionista. He understood the importance of feeling comfortable and confident in what you wear and he was always ready to give advice on choosing the right outfit. As we prepare for special occasions, let us remember Moses' wisdom and dress with confidence.

Get The Interview

Throughout his life, Moses had to prove himself to many. He had to prove himself to Pharaoh, the Israelites, and even God. But he never gave up and eventually achieved his goals. In this chapter, we will look at how Moses achieved his goals and how we can apply his teachings to get a job interview.

First, we must be prepared. Before Moses approached Pharaoh, he spoke with his brother Aaron and prepared himself for the task ahead. In the same way, preparation is essential for getting a job interview. Research the company you're applying to and develop an understanding of the job role and industry. Knowing what you're walking into will give you the confidence to perform well in an interview.

Second, be confident in yourself. Moses was sure of his purpose and never backed down. He believed in himself and his ability to get the job done. The same should be true for you. Believe in yourself and your abilities and let that confidence shine through in your job interview.

Third, be persistent. Moses was persistent in his approach to Pharaoh, and it eventually paid off. This same level of persistence should be applied when trying to get a job interview. Follow up with employers and show them that you are serious about getting an interview.

Finally, have faith. Moses had faith that God would be with him in his mission. You should have faith in yourself and your abilities. Believe that you will succeed and the job interview will be yours.

These are the teachings of Moses and how he achieved success. With faith, confidence, persistence, and preparation, you too can get that job interview. Remember the words of Moses: "Be strong and of good courage; do not be afraid, nor be dismayed, for the Lord your God is with you wherever you go." (Joshua 1:9)

Have Any Questions?

Moses is an exemplary figure in the Bible, known for his leadership, compassion, and wisdom. His journey to deliver the Israelites from slavery in Egypt is a testament to his unwavering faith and determination. When it comes to interviewing, Moses can serve as an excellent model of what to ask and not ask during an interview.

Questions They Might Ask During the Interview:

1. What do you believe makes you uniquely qualified for this role?

2. What do you see as the biggest challenges in this position?

3. How do you prefer to receive feedback?

4. What strategies have you used to successfully handle difficult tasks or situations?

5. How do you stay informed of changes in the industry?

Questions They Shouldn't Ask During the Interview:

1. What is your age?

2. What religion do you practice?

3. Are you married?

4. What political beliefs do you hold?

5. Do you have any children?

Moses's journey is a reminder that with faith and determination, anything is possible. Asking the right questions during an interview can help ensure that the right candidate is chosen for the position. Asking inappropriate questions can lead to legal issues and hurt the company's reputation. It is important to remember that the focus of an interview should be on the candidate's qualifications, not their personal life.

There are some great questions you should ask to make yourself stand out. Here are a few,

1. What makes this position unique from other similar roles?

2. What challenges or opportunities do you anticipate for this role?

3. What is the organizational culture like?

4. What are the expectations for the role and what metrics will be used to measure success?

5. What are the key performance indicators for this role?

6. How will I be supported in this role?

7. What are the career development opportunities for this role?

8. What would you consider to be the biggest accomplishments to date for this role?

9. What is the team dynamic like in this role?

10. How does this role fit into the larger organizational structure?

11. What are the key strategies for success in this role?

12. What kind of training and onboarding will I receive for this role?

13. What kind of feedback can I expect in this role?

14. How will my success be evaluated in this role?

15. What kind of skills and experience do you consider to be most important for this role?

16. What do you think is the most important factor for someone to be successful in this role?

17. What do you think Moses can bring to the role that other candidates can't?

18. What kind of challenges or problems will I be expected to solve in this role?

19. How will my contribution be measured in this role?

20. What kind of support will I have to help me succeed in this role?

Prepare For The Interview

Moses is a figure in the Bible known for his leadership and courage. As such, Moses provides a great example of what it takes to prepare for an interview. Here are a few tips from Moses for preparing for an interview.

1. Know Thyself: Moses was an exceptional leader because he had a deep understanding of his own strengths and weaknesses. Before an interview, it is important to understand your own skills and experiences and be able to articulate them clearly.

2. Research: Prior to his encounter with Pharaoh, Moses

researched the situation and had a plan for how to address it. Researching the company and position you are interviewing for is key to ensuring that you are able to answer questions and provide meaningful responses.

3. Practice: Moses was revered for his spoken eloquence and ability to persuade. The same is true for interviews. It is important to practice your responses so that you are comfortable and confident in the interview.

4. Be Prepared: Moses was known for his foresight and

planning. Before your interview, make sure you have all the necessary materials, such as resumes, references, and portfolios.

5. Be Confident: Despite the challenges presented to him, Moses was a leader who remained confident and unafraid. In an interview, confidence is key. Show the interviewer that you are the best candidate for the job.

We can learn a lot from Moses' example. By following the tips above, you will be able to prepare for your interview with confidence and poise.

Moses was a great leader and his experience gives us valuable insight into how to approach interview questions. In this chapter, we will explore how Moses might have answered common interview questions, and how we can use his wisdom to help us ace our own interviews.

1. Tell me about yourself?

Moses was a leader who was said to have spoken directly to God. He was a man of great strength, courage, and patience. He was a man of faith, and he had a strong sense of justice. He was a humble man who was willing to put his faith in God and follow his own convictions. He was a leader who was able to take charge in difficult situations, and he had the capacity to be a good listener.

When asked this question, Moses could have spoken about his leadership qualities, his faith, and his convictions. He could have discussed his experience as a leader and his willingness to put his trust in God. He could have also discussed his humility, his strength, and his willingness to take charge when needed.

2. What are your strengths and weaknesses?

Moses was a man of great strength and courage. He was a man of deep faith who was willing to put his trust in God and follow his own convictions. He was also a great listener and a leader who was able to take charge in difficult situations. However, he was also humble and had difficulty expressing his feelings.

When asked this question, Moses could have discussed his strengths, such as his faith, courage, and leadership abilities. He could have also discussed his humility and his difficulty expressing his feelings. He could have also discussed his willingness to put his trust in God and follow his convictions.

3. Why do you want this job?

Moses could have discussed his faith and his desire to use his experience and knowledge to help others. He could have also discussed his desire to lead and serve others. He could have also spoken about his desire to make a difference in the world and to use his strengths to help others.

When asked this question, Moses could have discussed his desire to lead, serve, and make a difference in the world. He could have also discussed his faith and his desire to use his experience and knowledge to help others.

Thank You

Moses was a great leader and mentor of the Israelites, and he was always mindful to express his gratitude to those who had helped his people. In today's world, writing thank you notes after interviews is just as important. In this chapter, we will explore how Moses would have written thank you notes after interviews and what he would have included.

Moses was a man of great humility and grace, so it's no surprise that he would have written thank you notes to employers after successful interviews. He would have taken the time to express his sincere appreciation for the opportunity to be considered for the position and to thank the employer for taking time out of their day to speak with him.

Moses would have also taken the opportunity to express his enthusiasm for the position and reiterate his qualifications for the job. He would have offered to answer any follow-up questions and included his contact information so the employer could reach out to him. Finally, he would have ended the letter with a sincere thank you and a willingness to stay in touch.

Moses would have made sure to include specific details from the interview in his thank you notes. He would have mentioned topics of conversation that resonated with him, topics that he found interesting, and any advice or opinions he received during the interview. Moses would have also expressed his enthusiasm for the position and his commitment to his role if he got the job.

Moses would have also been sure to thank the interviewer for their time and consideration. He would have done this in a thoughtful and sincere way, expressing his gratitude for the opportunity to be considered for the job. Finally, Moses would have asked if there was any additional information he could provide that would strengthen his candidacy. By doing this, he would have shown the employer that he was interested in the job and was willing to go the extra mile to stand out from the competition.

In conclusion, Moses would have written thank you notes to employers after successful interviews that were thoughtful, sincere, and included specific details from the interview. He would have thanked the interviewer for their time and consideration, expressed his enthusiasm for the position, and conveyed his commitment to the role if he got the job.

As someone who has been remembered throughout history for his leadership, I understand the importance of showing gratitude and appreciation for the kindness and generosity of others. Here are some tips for writing an effective thank you note to express your sincere appreciation:

1. Make sure to include the name of the person you are thanking in

the note. This will help ensure that the recipient knows exactly who is expressing their gratitude.

2. Make sure to express your gratitude in a heartfelt and sincere way. A thank you note should be more than just a formality; it should be a reflection of how much you appreciate the kindness and generosity you have received.

3. Use language that is respectful and appropriate. It is important to use language that conveys the proper level of respect for the recipient.

4. Keep the note short and to the point. While it is important to express your gratitude, it is also important to be concise and to the point.

5. Make sure to include a signature at the end of the note. A signature is an important way to show that you are taking the time to personally thank the recipient.

Following these tips will help ensure that your thank you note conveys your gratitude in the most effective and meaningful way. Thanking others for their kindness and generosity is an important part of showing appreciation and respect, and these tips will help ensure that your message is conveyed in the most sincere and heartfelt way.

Economically Challenged Hunters

In the Bible, the story of Moses is one of courage and

strength in the face of adversity. Born into slavery, Moses was raised by his adoptive parents and eventually called by God to lead the Israelites out of captivity in Egypt. Although Moses faced many obstacles and trials along the way, his ultimate success in leading the Israelites to freedom serves as an inspiration to those who are homeless looking for a job.

This chapter will explore the lessons we can learn from Moses' story and how to overcome feelings of hopelessness and fear that come with being homeless and looking for a job.

The first lesson we can learn from Moses' story is that faith can make all the difference. Even when faced with seemingly insurmountable odds, Moses held onto his faith in God and never gave up. This faith gave him the strength to overcome his fears and ultimately led him to success.

The second lesson we can learn from Moses' story is the importance of perseverance. Despite the many challenges he faced, Moses never gave up and kept pushing forward. This determination enabled him to stay focused on his goal and ultimately achieve it.

The third lesson we can learn from Moses' story is that trusting in God is essential. Moses constantly turned to God for guidance and support and never wavered in his faith. This trust in God helped him to stay on course and provided him with the strength to face even the toughest of obstacles. Ultimately, Moses's unwavering faith in God was what enabled him to achieve his goals.

Finally, Moses' story teaches us that even when we feel alone and without hope, help is always available. God provided Moses with assistance in the form of his brother Aaron and sister Miriam who were with him every step of the way

We can also learn from Moses' story that persistence is key. He did not give up when things got difficult; instead, he kept pushing forward and kept his eyes on the prize. This same kind of persistence is essential for those who are homeless and looking for a job. Even when the odds seem insurmountable, it is important to keep pushing forward and never give up.

The third lesson we can learn from Moses' story is that it is important to reach out for help when needed. When Moses was unable to lead the Israelites out of Egypt on his own, he reached out to his brother, Aaron, for assistance. Reaching out for help is a critical step for those who are homeless and looking for a job. There are many organizations and resources available to help homeless individuals, and it is important to take advantage of these resources and not be afraid to ask for help.

Finally, we can learn from Moses' story that resilience is essential. Despite the difficulties and obstacles Moses faced, he was able to stay strong and overcome them. This same kind of resilience is key for those who are homeless and looking for a job. It is important to stay focused on the goal and never give up in the face of adversity. It is also important to remember that seeking help is not a sign of weakness. On the contrary, it is a sign of strength and determination. By reaching out for assistance, we can leverage our own individual resources and combine them with those of the organizations and resources that are available. This will provide a greater chance of success in finding a job and improving our lives. Ultimately, it is up to each individual to take the necessary steps to become self-sufficient and to break the cycle of homelessness.

In conclusion, Moses' story serves as a beacon of hope and inspiration to those who are homeless and looking for a job. By following his example, we can learn the importance of faith, persistence, reaching out for help, and resilience in overcoming feelings of hopelessness and fear. These are the very traits that will help us to take charge of our lives and move forward in the best way possible. With the right mix of determination and assistance, lasting change is possible. We can all learn from Moses' journey and use it to empower ourselves and our communities.

Job interviews can be difficult for anyone, but for homeless people, they can be especially intimidating. Homelessness can leave individuals feeling ashamed and lacking in the resources they need to make a great impression in a job interview. Fortunately, there are organizations and resources that can help homeless people prepare for job interviews and make the most of their opportunities.

Showers and Clean Clothing

One of the most important aspects of preparing for a job interview is personal hygiene. Homeless people often struggle to access basic necessities such as showers and clean clothes. Fortunately, there are organizations that provide these services at no cost. For example, some shelters provide showers and laundry services for homeless people. Other organizations provide free clothing donations so that homeless people can look their best for job interviews.

Resume Assistance

Having a well-crafted resume can make a big difference in the job search process. Unfortunately, many homeless people lack the resources to create a professional resume. Luckily, there are organizations that offer free resume assistance to homeless people. These organizations provide coaching on how to create an effective resume, as well as advice on how to present it to potential employers.

Helpful Organizations

There are many organizations dedicated to helping homeless people prepare for job interviews. For example, the National Coalition for the Homeless offers job-readiness training, resume assistance, and even job-placement services to homeless people. The Homeless Assistance Network provides free career counseling, job search assistance, and other services to homeless people. And the National Alliance to End Homelessness offers a variety of job-readiness programs, including job-interview coaching and resume-writing workshops.

The resources available to homeless people for preparing for job interviews vary from state to state. It is important to research local organizations that can provide assistance. With the right resources, homeless people can gain the confidence and skills they need to make a great impression in job interviews. Additionally, there are many organizations that provide employment and job-training programs for homeless people. For instance, the United Way often partners with local organizations to offer job-training courses and employment workshops that are tailored to the needs of the homeless community.

These programs can help homeless people gain the skills and qualifications needed to secure a job. Additionally, many homeless shelters provide support to those who are actively seeking employment. These shelters can provide assistance with the job

search process, including help
with writing resumes, mock
interviews.

I Want A Better Job

Moses was a great leader and role model for all of us. He was called by God to lead the Israelites out of Egypt and into the Promised Land. As such, he had to be up-to-date on the latest trends in career advancement and job seeking. Below are a few tips for job seekers upgrading their careers, inspired by the life of Moses:

1. Stay focused on your goals: Moses was a man of great focus and determination. He didn't let any distractions get in the way of his mission to lead the Israelites

out of Egypt. Job seekers should stay focused on their goals and objectives in order to make sure their efforts don't go to waste.

2. Utilize your network: Moses had a strong network of supporters both in Egypt and in the Promised Land. When he needed help or guidance, he was able to turn to his network for support. Job seekers should also utilize their personal and professional networks to find new opportunities and build relationships.

3. Take risks: Moses took a big risk in leading the Israelites out of Egypt and into the Promised Land. He had to make some tough decisions and take some chances in order to succeed. Job seekers should also be willing to take risks in order to get ahead and reach their goals.

4. Don't be afraid to ask for help: Moses wasn't afraid to ask for help when he needed it. He wasn't ashamed of his limitations, and he was willing to turn to God and his friends for guidance. Job seekers should also be willing to ask for help when necessary.

5. Persevere: Moses faced many obstacles and setbacks on his journey to the Promised Land. But he never gave up and he persevered until the end. Job seekers should also learn to persevere and never give up, even in the face of adversity.

By following these tips, inspired by Moses, job seekers can upgrade their careers and reach their goals.

Moses was a great leader in the Bible, and his story can provide important guidance for job seekers today. In this chapter, we'll explore some special considerations for job seekers inspired by Moses' story.

First, Moses demonstrated great determination, even when faced with difficult challenges. He persevered against all odds in his pursuit of his goals, and this is an important lesson for job seekers. One should not give up easily on a job search but should continually strive towards their desired career.

Second, Moses was an effective communicator. He was able to clearly articulate his needs and desires to those he encountered. Job seekers should also be sure to practice strong communication skills when applying for jobs or interviewing. Being able to clearly express oneself is key in an effective job search.

Third, Moses was a great listener. He was willing to hear what other people had to say, and this enabled him to be more successful in his endeavors. Job seekers should also be sure to listen to potential employers and be open to their feedback. This can be a great way to make a positive impression and stand out in the job search process.

Finally, Moses was a leader, and he was able to motivate those around him. Job seekers should strive to be a leader in their job search. They should remain positive and show determination, which can motivate them to reach their goals.

Moses' story is an inspiring one, and his example can help guide job seekers in their endeavors. Job seekers should remember his determination, communication skills, listening abilities, and leadership qualities when pursuing their desired career. With these special considerations, job seekers can be successful in their job search.

Conclusion

Moses was a man of great faith and a leader of his people. He was a man of God who led the Israelites out of slavery in Egypt and into the Promised Land. Moses was a wise and knowledgeable leader, and he understood the importance of preparing for the future. He showed this wisdom when he set up the Ten Commandments as a way to ensure that his people could live a life of justice and righteousness. He also gave them laws and instructions on how they should live in order to be good citizens of the nation.

In addition, Moses also gave them the insight to trust in God as their provider and protector. His legacy of faith and leadership still lives on today, and he is remembered as one of the greatest figures in Jewish history.

In this chapter, Moses shares his advice for finding a job. He states that it is important to be prepared and to stay focused on the goal. He recommends researching the job market, networking with contacts, and creating a professional resume. Moses also stresses the importance of confidence and perseverance. He encourages job seekers to never give up and to keep trying even when the going gets tough.

Moses also encourages job seekers to think about the skills they have to offer and to identify ways to enhance them. He reminds readers that it is important to be honest and to take the time to understand the job they are applying for so that they can present themselves in the best light. Finally, he advises job seekers to take advantage of the resources available to them, such as job fairs, career centers, and online job search websites.

He believes that these resources provide valuable information and support that can help job seekers find success. With the right preparation and attitude, Moses believes that any job seeker can find the job they are looking for.

Moses stresses the importance of networking to job seekers as well. He believes that making connections with people in the industry can be a powerful tool in the job search process. He suggests reaching out to friends, family, and colleagues for assistance in finding job leads and offers of advice.

He also recommends joining professional organizations and

attending career events and networking functions to expand one's job search horizons. In addition, Moses encourages job seekers to utilize social media to get their name out there and to make connections

In addition, Moses advises job seekers to have a plan for dealing with rejection. He encourages them to stay positive, to find strength in the experience, and to use it as an opportunity to learn and grow. Finally, he encourages job seekers to take the time to enjoy the process, because the journey to finding a job can be just as important as the destination.

Moses' advice is timeless and still applicable today. He reminds us that the job search process can be difficult, but with the right attitude and preparation, success is within reach. Moses also encourages job seekers to practice self-care throughout the process. He suggests taking the time to relax and enjoy life - to get out and do something that brings joy. This helps to maintain a healthy balance between job searching and personal life.

Additionally, Moses recommends job seekers to stay organized and to create a schedule that allows them to stay on track with their job search. Taking the time to plan and prioritize tasks will help job seekers stay focused and motivated.

Searching for a job can be a daunting task, and it is important to make sure you are gathering all the information you need to make the best decision. It is important to utilize a variety of resources when searching for a job; here are some of the most helpful sources for job seeking information:

1. Online job boards – Online job boards such as Indeed and Monster are great places to start when searching for jobs. You can create a profile and upload your resume, and search for jobs in the location and field of your choice.

2. LinkedIn – LinkedIn is a powerful networking tool that allows you to connect with other professionals in your field and search for jobs. You can also create a professional profile and showcase your skills and experience.

3. Local newspapers and job fairs – Many local newspapers advertise job openings in the area, and job fairs are also a great way to meet potential employers.

4. Networking – Networking is one of the most important parts of job searching. Connect with professionals in your field and ask for advice and referrals.

5. Professional organizations – Joining a professional organization can be a great way to make connections and learn about job openings.

6. Social media – Many employers use social media to advertise job openings and connect with potential hires.

7. College career centers – If you are a recent graduate, your college career center is a great resource for job searching. Many career centers offer one-on-one counseling, resume reviews, and job-search workshops.

By utilizing all of these sources, you can be sure to find the best job for you. Good luck in your job search!

Drew Wohlford always had dreams of becoming a script writer but then life happened. His parents divorced shortly after high school, he attended St Francis College in Fort Wayne, Indiana after wandering aimlessly in life for years. Again he found his passion for writing after being encouraged by Dr. L. Carl

 Nadeau, his creative writing teacher.

Then life happene d again, he met his wife, Brenda. Soon there were kids, and then grandkids. There were numerous jobs of all kinds, as he tried to find his passion, but it had been put on a back burner. Then in November of 2020 Drew was hit with Covid, which turned into long covid and without work, and facing his 60th birthday, Drew didn't look back, he looked forward and thought, it's now or never. With laptop in hand, he began to document the stories he told his grandchildren. The passion had once again been ignited.

Discover These Other Great Books
By Author Drew Wohlford on AMAZON

Discover These Other Great Books
By Author Drew Wohlford on AMAZON
THE LENS
He got a good deal on a camera lens that might land him in prison for life.
Drew Wohlford
THE CRAIGSLIST AD
Andrew Wohlford
MADE IN CHINA
Drew Wohlford
HELP!
I can't figure out the best platform to write on.
Pro's and cons of popular writing platforms
Drew Wohlford
George Russo's
Best Pizza
Recipes
"The secret is in the sauce"
Drew Wohlford
MRS. PRESZINGLE AND THE CURIOUS TREASURE
DREW WOHLFORD
February 15th
DREW WOHLFORD
DEARLY DEMENTED
Drew Wohlford
ODBODY
The Humble Clockmaker
Drew Wohlford
Breakfast On The Beach
365 Devotionals to get closer to Jesus
Drew Wohlford
Like A Country Song
Drew Wohlford
Bodies In The Backyard
My First 60 Years
Drew Wohlford
An Autobiography

Discover These Other Great Books
By Author Drew Wohlford on AMAZON